Thomas Edgar McNally is a mentor, educator, songwriter, and story-teller who celebrates life, family, and friends on his *Refrigerator Door*.

The mosaic of happiness!

REFRIGERATOR DOOR

Thomas Edgar McNally

AUSTIN MACAULEY PUBLISHERS™

Ordering Information
Quantity sales: Special discounts are available on quantity purchases by corporations, associations, and others. For details, contact the publisher at the address below.

Publisher's Cataloging-in-Publication data
McNally, Thomas Edgar
Refrigerator Door

ISBN 9798886937039 (Paperback)
ISBN 9798886937046 (Hardback)
ISBN 9798886937060 (ePub e-book)
ISBN 9798886937053 (Audiobook)

Library of Congress Control Number: 2023923067

www.austinmacauley.com/us

First Published 2024
Austin Macauley Publishers LLC
40 Wall Street, 33rd Floor, Suite 3302
New York, NY 10005
USA

mail-usa@austinmacauley.com
+1 (646) 5125767

Edna Simpson, HELP from Georgia, worked for our family, who taught me to celebrate life on the *Refrigerator Door*!

Gary Floto, special friend, Vietnam war hero, used our Refrigerator Door as a place to post photos! RIP!

C. Patrick Allen, a friend, mentor, and hero – RIP

Glenn Lau, "Message in a bottle…" RIP!

Lester, my SOULMATE. FOREVER TOGETHER, inspired me to write, sing, compose, and celebrate!

McNally – Dunne – Sullivan – Winstanley – Flanders – Irish Families!

Ferris State University, Big Rapids, Michigan, USA

Western Michigan University Kalamazoo, Michigan, USA

Brooke Uzarski,

Graphic Communication Instructor.

Kent Career Technical Center.

1655 E. Beltline Ave. NE

Grand Rapids, MI 49525

616-802-3618

brookeuzarski@kentisd.org

Kate Nelson, student, KCTC,

Illustration contributions.

My grandkids sitting around, having "flap-jacks" with bananas, sharing Edna's memory and the history of the Refrigerator Door…! Life at my lodge. Going back in time, each grandchild's memory. Photos, art, magnets, political stickers, schedules, reminders and recipes. Our celebration of family life.

Life at the lodge! A place of comfort and sharing. All memories, reminders, important numbers, ideas,

calendar dates are on the Refrigerator Door!

    Funny photos and great memories are always posted and forever changing!

My Refrigerator Door!

The Refrigerator Door allows all to share, brag, post, schedule, communicate, remind, and guide us through life. Posted 'great sayings' can give us inspiration on a daily, monthly, yearly and forever basis. Quotes can help us feel we can take on life's many challenges. The Refrigerator Door helps us to remember all that is important!

"Papa, so why Teddy Roosevelt on the Refrigerator Door?"

"Well, my grandfather, the man I am named after, the first Tommy Ed, was a soldier with Teddy Roosevelt.

He was a Rough Rider who fought a war in Cuba.

"Soon to be President of the United States of America, Roosevelt had many great sayings. Teddy, as he was called, was an inspiration to my grandfather, the country and to this very day, to the world! He was an exceptional leader, man and environmentalist. He was very dedicated to preserving nature."

In life and in death, Teddy Roosevelt, a mentor to the world!

C. Patrick Allen RIP

"Who is this big fella all dressed in camo?"

"That's my friend, Dr. Pat, who sadly died a few years ago. Pat was a great man, kind of like a Teddy Roosevelt. He loved the mountains and he, too, harvested his own food."

"Kind'a like us!" one of the grandkids chimed in. "We eat the fish we catch, and the turkey and deer, we hunt."

"So very true, plus, we eat the morel mushrooms,

fiddleheads, and wild leeks."

Lots of our recipes are posted on the Refrigerator Door!

"Hey Papa, don't forget you hang signs on the Refrigerator Door that remind us not to eat ice-cream!" added one of the grandkids.

"Most importantly," Papa added. "I have already begun each of your future Refrigerator Doors! Just look at the pictures of you guys when you were young. A tribute to your sister, who is now an angel. A memorial to my mom, your great-grandmother, who you kids called, 'Candy Lady'. Each time we visited her, she always had treats.

"I have your school photos posted and I change them each year."

"Papa, how did all of this begin? We love seeing our photos of adventures on the Refrigerator Door! It tells

us how you find it so very important to showcase our time together.”

The four grandkids carefully look at the postings on the Refrigerator Door.

“Hey, look at my art from long ago!”

“Well, look at the big fish we caught, plus it was a delicious treat!” Exclaimed one of the grandkids. Her sister pointed at the picture of the fish. So, it’s memory is on the Refrigerator Door. And the tasty dinner was inside the refrigerator. A very special time and memory – forever cherished and celebrated.

Trout fishing memories, plus nice reminders of how we take pride in the way we look. “That’s a crazy photo of us dressed up," one chimed in.

The Refrigerator Door allows us to celebrate holidays and special occasions. Just look at this halloween photo!

"Papa, you are goofy!" exclaimed one of the kids.

"Always! Life is too short not to laugh. That's why I try to post smiley faces, jokes, cute photos and other things on the Refrigerator Door that bring smiles on other's faces. Each and every day needs to begin with a smile and a laugh.

Again, remember, the Refrigerator Door feeds our

mind, heart and soul. The refrigerator feeds our body."

Big eyes! Halloween tricks and Fun memory!

Being funny on Halloween with friend!!!!

Outdoor adventure success photos all

"So how did you learn to use the Refrigerator Door for sharing your special memories and accomplishments?"

The grandkids all exclaimed. Curiosity was painted on their faces. All waited in silence hoping for an answer.

"Well, for me, as I was learning to read. My first report card from kindergarten was posted on the door by my mom.

"Then, my grandmother, who lived with us, would post my colorings. My dad would post pictures of the fish that we used to catch. My brother would post his report cards.

"Edna Simpson, as she made me special lunches on school days, would post whatever school work I may had brought home.

"The very first baseball team I was on, the UTES, was a big photo that took center stage one summer."

"Papa, what's a UTES?"

"Great question! All of the teams were named after Indian tribes. The UTES was a tribe that lived in the area surrounding the state of Mississippi."

"So, Papa, kind'a like our grandmother, who is an Indian, your baseball team was named after a great tribe of Indians."

"Yes!"

"My dad, Robert Sr. would take me and my brother fishing. We never caught much but my dad always

taught us that we eat what we harvest. On this trip, we had fried blue gill and home-made french fries for lunch. Yummy!

"Sports teams are often named after great things in history. As you can see, our family's logo is proudly displayed always, on the Refrigerator Door!

"Our American and Irish ancestry brings the greatness that always deserves much celebration and pride.

"Going back in time, my first report card, posted on the Refrigerator Door, began a focus on trying to do my best in school and be proud of my accomplishments. To this very day, I post on the Refrigerator Door all of my accomplishments while in school. And yes, colleges

and universities are schools. Best of life is to always share, learn and be proud. Displaying what you have accomplished and earned gives you the motivation to 'keep up and keep going on…!'

"The perfect place to post, share and highlight, awards, accomplishments, graduations, special photos, gifts and so much more. As the saying goes, 'The sky is the limit!' Which means, there is no limit to what one might post, hang or share.

"Here's the very logo of my most favorite university; Ferris State University. Their mascot is the bulldog, so it hangs on the Refrigerator Door!

Ferris State University

"Especially if you have magnetic or sticky numbers and letters, messages, sayings and reminders then options are always fluid as they can be changed daily.

"I like to use chip clip magnets, small pieces of tape that is rolled up and magnets that I get from politicians, businesses or ones that I buy myself.

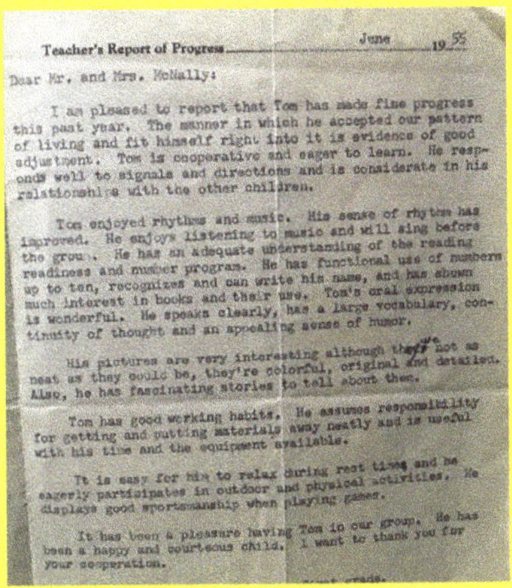

Papa Thom's first Report Card….posted on the Refrigerator Door !

"Showcasing those who influence your life, plus,

those who have special, motivational messages, definitely deserve a spot on the Refrigerator Door!"

Here are some of the "great ones" that I have had the pleasure of knowing.

Jerome Bettis, Super Bowl football star and Youth Advocate

Somers and Papa Thom

THE GREATEST! Ali inspired Papa to help others!

Michael Pritchard having a funny moment with

Papa Thom

Funny memory of special Sugar Corn Pops cereal for

Papa Thom!

Papa Thom and pro football star Rich Strenger

Jesse White Team working with Papa to motivate

youth!

"Papa, you seem so small!"

"Well, not really, it is just a reality that many sports stars are huge, tall people. What makes a person truly unique and special is the proverbial 'size of their heart!' I try to roll out my passions, likes, memories, great sayings and caring for others on the Refrigerator Door! It is the perfect place to celebrate life, remind yourself of things to do, to make, to eat and to remember. It is the perfect 'canvas of life!' Signs of expression, sharing and caring makes us all tall.

"Look at my basketball team members. We are all pretty close in height."

Papa Thom with basketball buddies!

Victory photos always on the Refrigerator Door!

"So, Papa, what are the most special postings you put on your Refrigerator Door?"

"Well, mine are always about family. Going back in time, photos of my grandparents, my parents, my kids and their kids. So, the Refrigerator Door becomes a map through time. A place of true celebration of the passing of time, as we remember it.

"As the saying goes, 'A picture is worth a thousand words…' The Refrigerator Door, like the mirror reflection of a pond, reflects what's important in our lives!

"Family, friends, pets and things we like. A true mosaic that speaks to our souls and tells others what we consider to be truly important."

Dublin!

2/24/2012 – 5/17/2012

Frankie McNally… RIP!

McNally "grandparents" and McNally-Goward kids…

Joseph C. McNally, my grandfather, and his 5 daughters and Mary Jane Flanders…soon to be a McNally and my mother!

May 1st Snow Storm

Moments in time that are hard to forget…lol!

McNallys catching salmon together!

Kids with their kids! Goward-Valentine-McNally!

Family and fun times!

McNally wedding: Margaret "Susie" Sullivan McNally attended

Charlie McNally

Stephen Thomas McNally

So, what's your story? What do you want to remember? Any appointments or goals? What do you think others might want to learn about you as they approach the Refrigerator Door?

Better than a laptop. More visible than a tablet or phone. The Refrigerator Door is the very gateway to sharing, organizing, remembering and even communicating to those close to you.

More than time to get your thoughts and shares organized and post, on the Refrigerator Door!

Develop themes. Make it seasonal. Celebrate holidays. Watch yourself grow!

Look at me over the years…

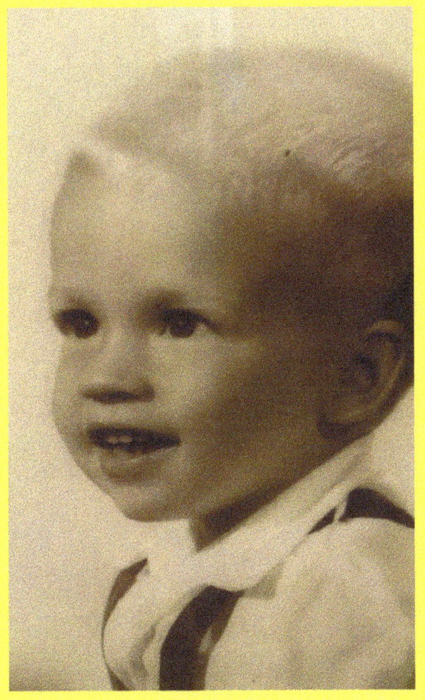

First photo!

Being a cowboy!

Hanging with the kids!

Papa Thom trophy photo!

Papa Thom Refrigerator Door outdoorsman photo!

Thomas E. McNally, 1949 – and still going strong!

To be continued…

What's your story?

Art

Photos

Reminders

Jokes

Magnets

Report cards

Certificates

Licenses

Anything you think is important!

Go for it! Start creating great memories daily, monthly, weekly, yearly!

E
A+
D
ROUTE
66
A B C
June
14
Get
Milk
HAPPY
I
J
Feed
Dog
K
food
water

E
A+
June 14
A
B
C
D
ROUTE 66
HAPPY
Ki

HAPPY
Recipe   Flapjacks
1/2
4
5
Get

E
D
A+
A B C
Route
66
May
10
Get
Milk
HAPPY
I
J
Feed
Dog
Ki
Food
Water

Sugar
flour
G
A+
June
14
ABC
ROUTE
66
D
Get
Milk
E
HAPPY
B+
K
I
U
Forever
Together

E
A+
May
10
A
B
C
Route
66
D
K G A F

FISH

THE
END

sugar
flour
G
A+
May
6
route
66
A B C
D
4
E
HAPPY
Get
Milk
B+
I
U
Ki

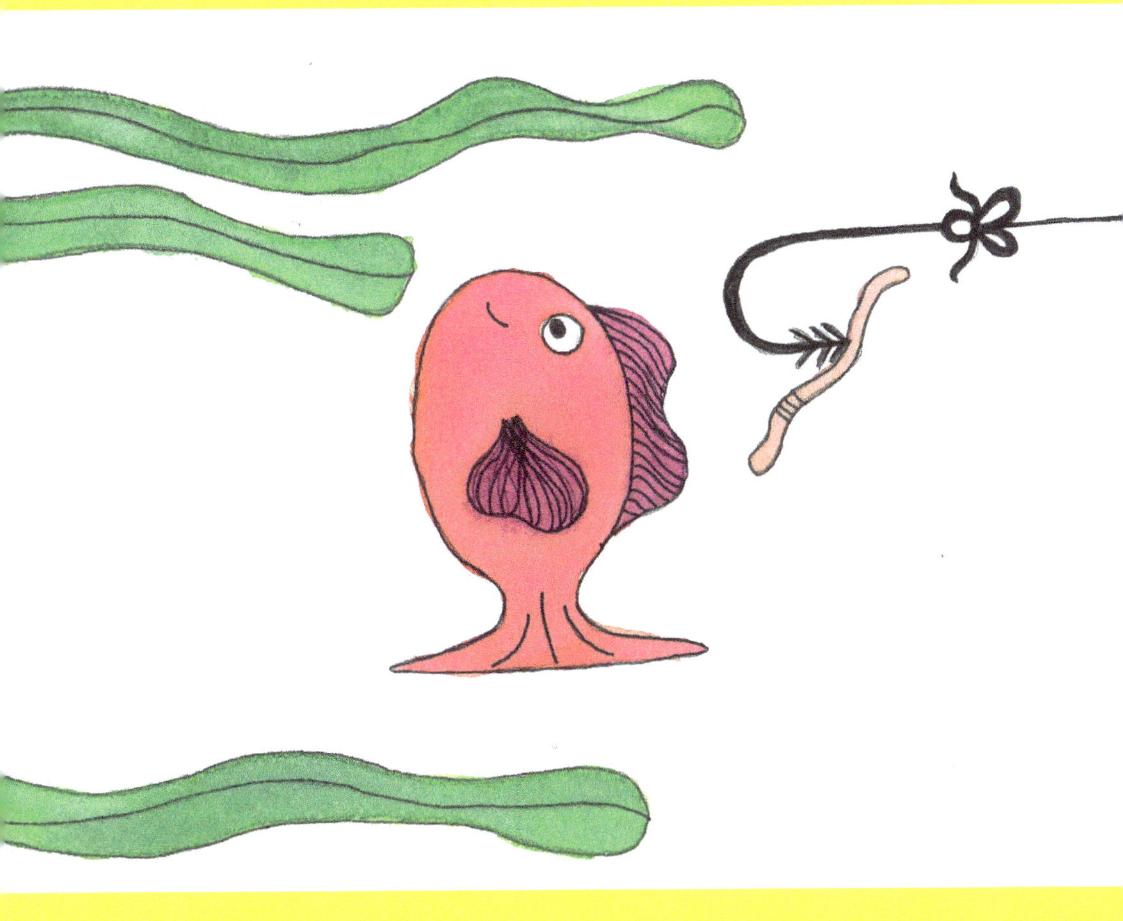

HAPP
Recipes   FlapJacks
Get Milk

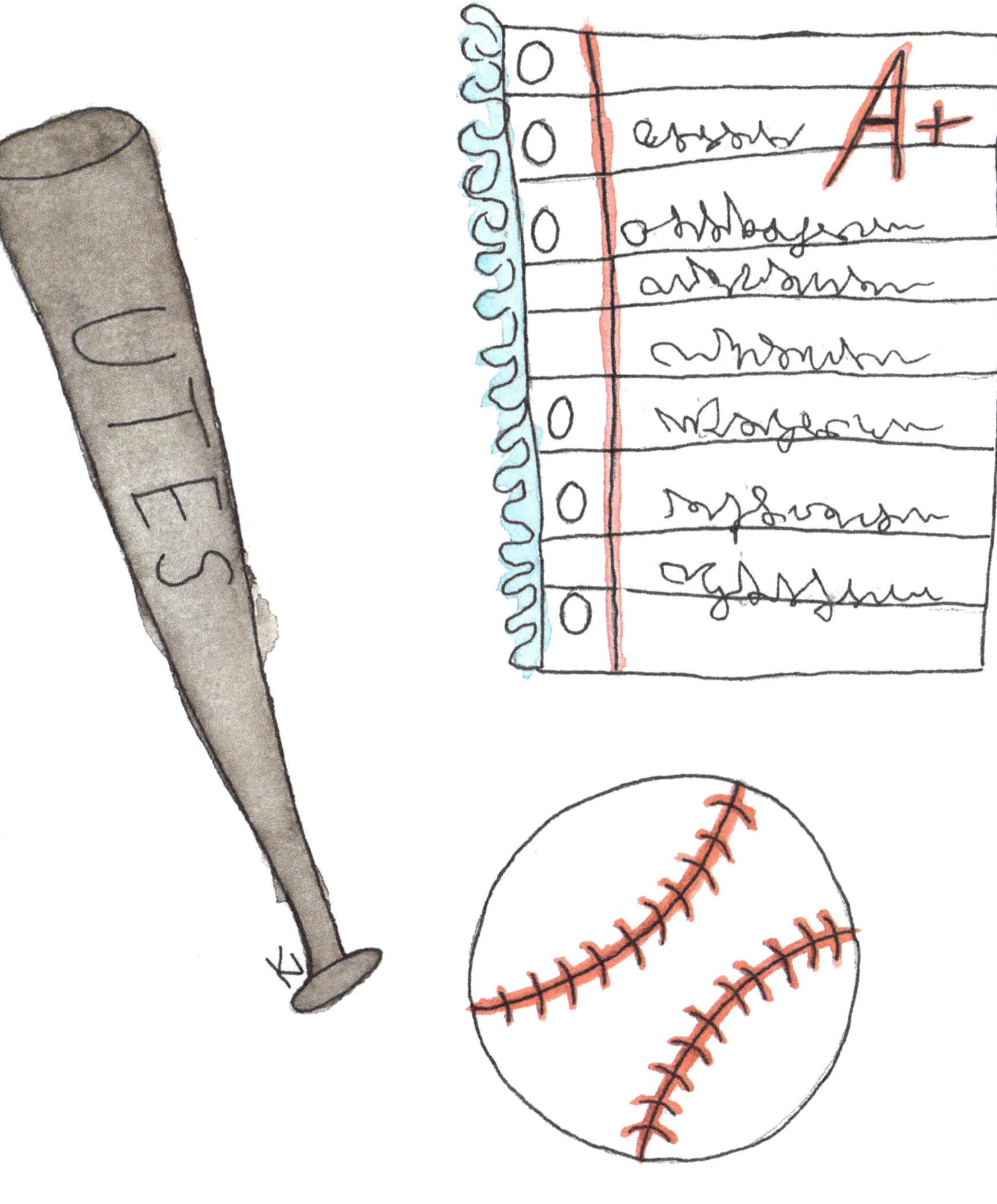

UTES
A+

BE HAPPY
Smile
Joy
KI

Milk

FISH

THE
END

UTES